Working Together Is Fun

by Benjamin Day
illustrated by Jean Morin

Scott Foresman
is an imprint of

Glenview, Illinois • Boston, Massachusetts • Mesa, Arizona
Shoreview, Minnesota • Upper Saddle River, New Jersey

Illustrations
Jean Morin

Photographs
Every effort has been made to secure permission and provide appropriate credit for photographic material. The publisher deeply regrets any omission and pledges to correct errors called to its attention in subsequent editions.

Unless otherwise acknowledged, all photographs are the property of Pearson Education, Inc.

12 ©Dylan Ellis/Getty Images

ISBN 13: 978-0-328-39369-5
ISBN 10: 0-328-39369-X

1 2 3 4 5 6 7 8 9 10 V010 17 16 15 14 13 12 11 10 09 08

Simon and his friends didn't like how their playground looked.

"We should plant flowers. They'll be pretty," said Anna.

"That's certainly a great idea," said Simon. "We'll need to buy tools."

"What can we do to earn money?" asked Simon.

"We could rake leaves," said Anna.

"I want to wash cars," said Mike.

"You're all wrong," argued Mary. "We should sell either used toys or games!"

Nobody could agree on how to raise money.

The friends were angry.

"I don't want to argue," said Simon. "I'm going home."

Simon stomped home.

"What's wrong, Simon?" asked his father.

"I had the worst day," Simon said.

He told his father about the argument.

"Maybe there's a way to solve this," said his father. "You can do all of those things. Why don't you make a plan?"

Simon called his friends together after school.

"We all want to plant flowers, right?" he asked. "Let's make a plan that will make us happy."

"But we all want to do different things," said Mike.

"Why can't we do all of those things?" asked Anna.

"Yes, all of those things could be fun," agreed Mary.

Simon started a list. "First we'll do yard work," he said.

"The second week we'll sell used toys or games," said Anna.

"Then we'll wash cars," said Mary.

"That's a great plan!" said Mike.

The friends started to do yard work.

"This is fun!" said Mike with a laugh.

"Having a sale next week will be fun too," said Anna.

Simon was glad they had solved their problem. They all had a good time working together.

Boys and Girls Clubs of America

The Boys and Girls Clubs of America offer kids the chance to grow and learn together. Clubs are located all over the United States, in cities as well as small towns. The clubs are open for all kids who want fun and friendship. Helpful teenagers and adults volunteer their time to lead the kids in different activities.

Kids can have fun playing and working together at these clubs. They can play sports and work on crafts. They can play music and dance. They can learn about nature and the world they live in. Sometimes they work together to help other people.

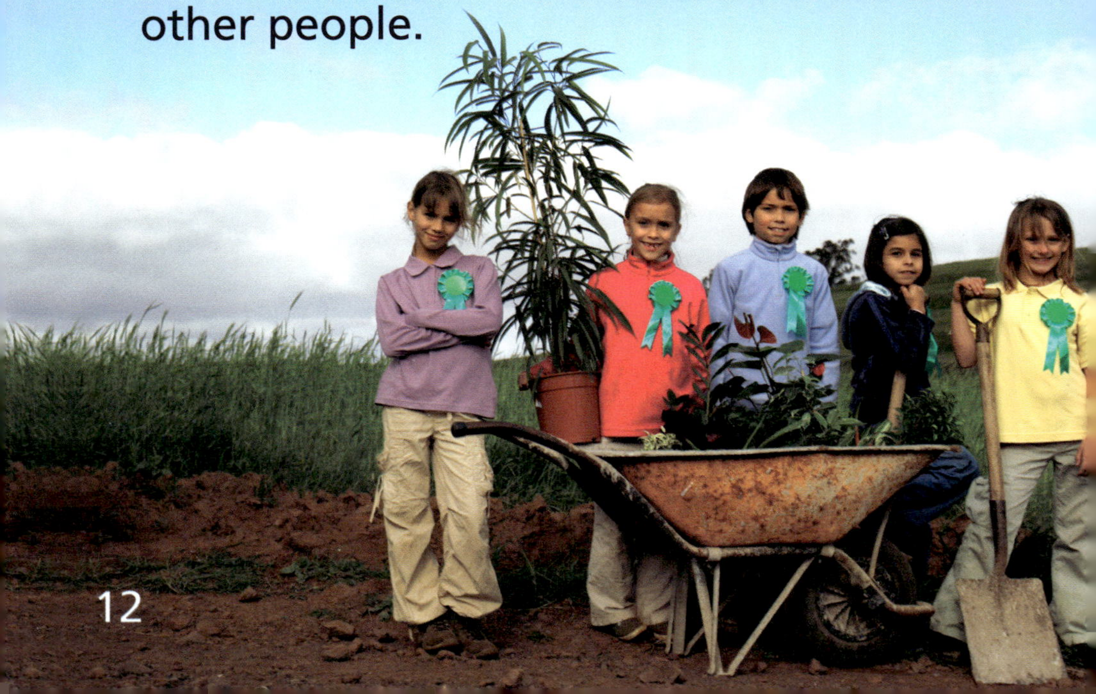